HALLOWEEN Memory BOOK

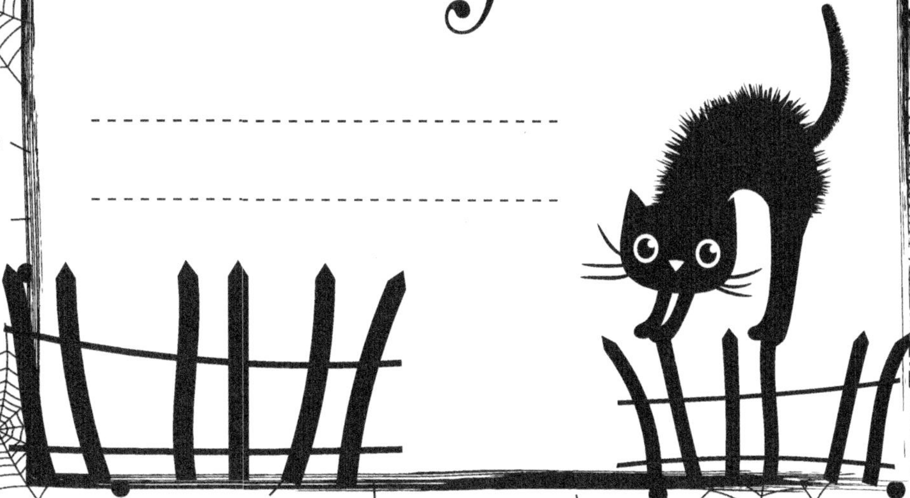

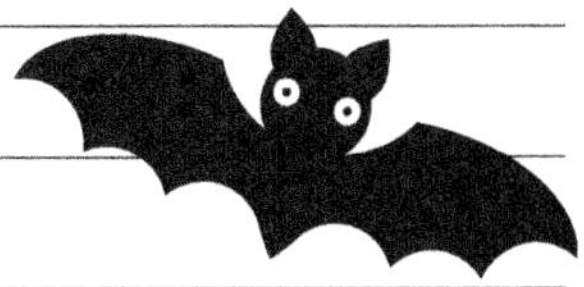

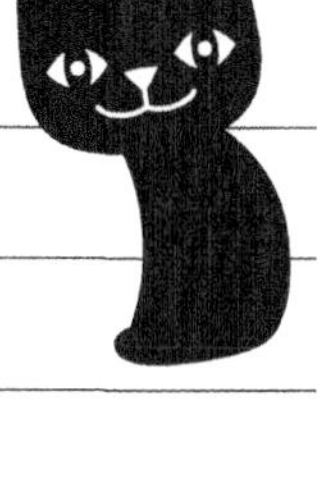

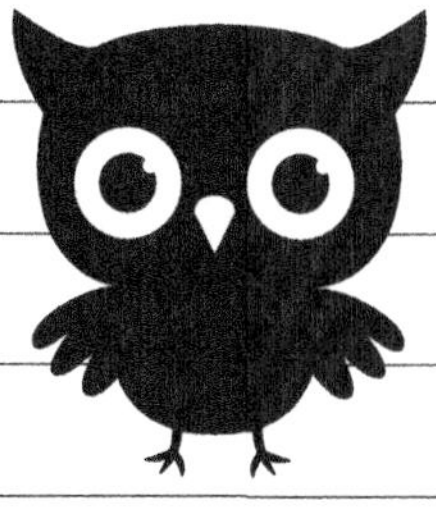

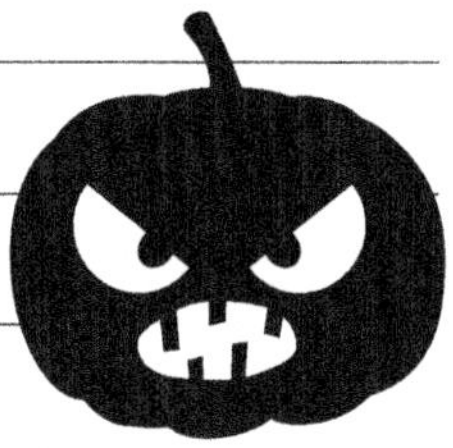

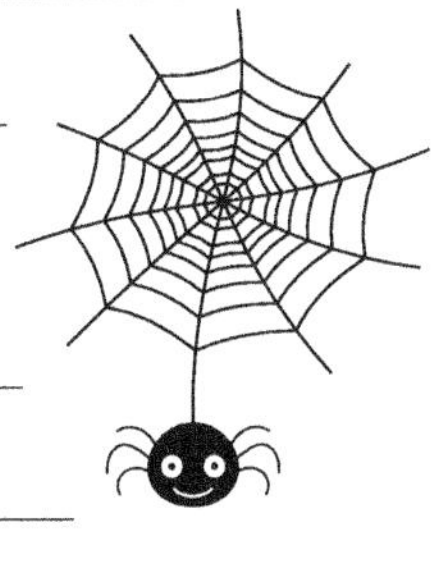

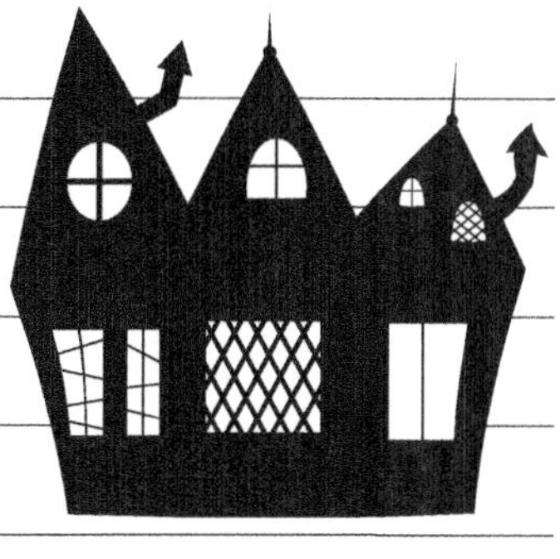

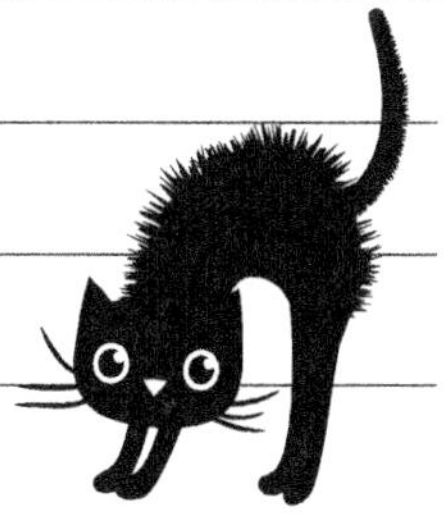

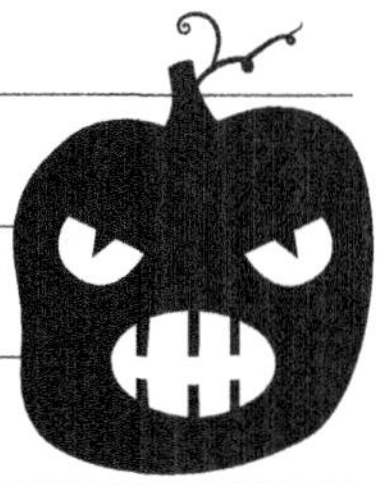

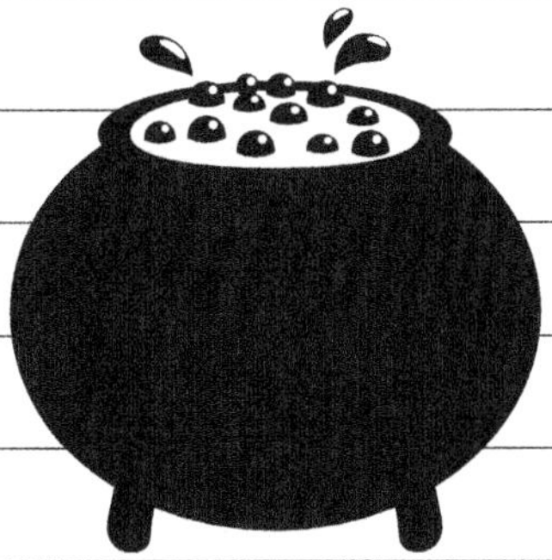

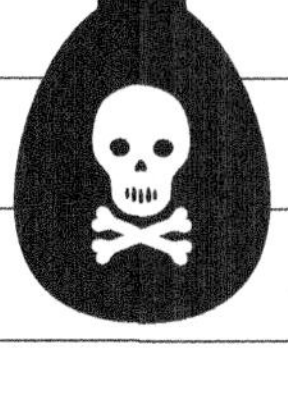

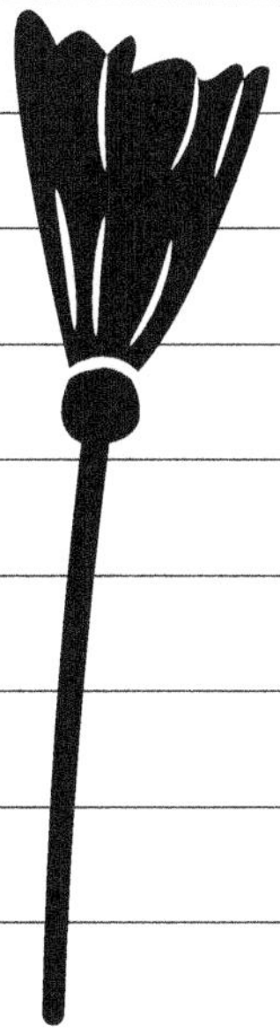

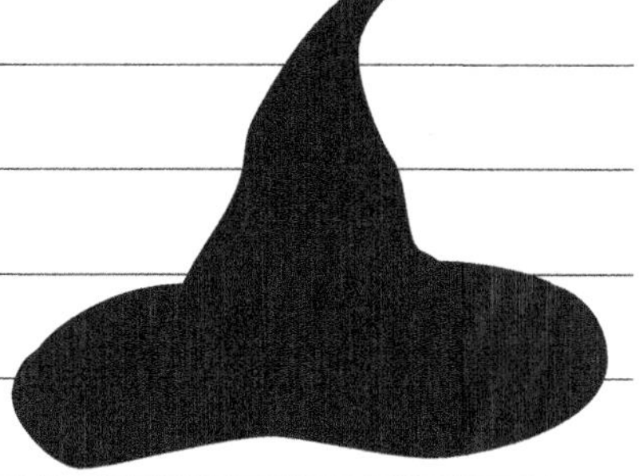

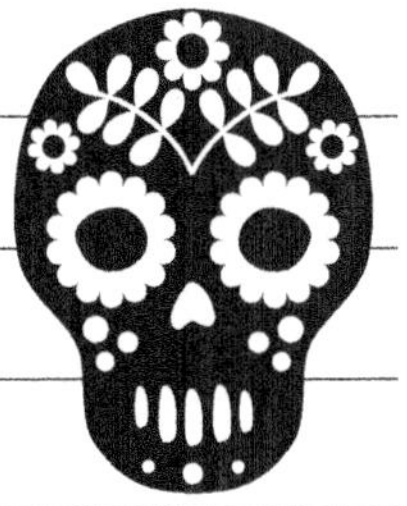

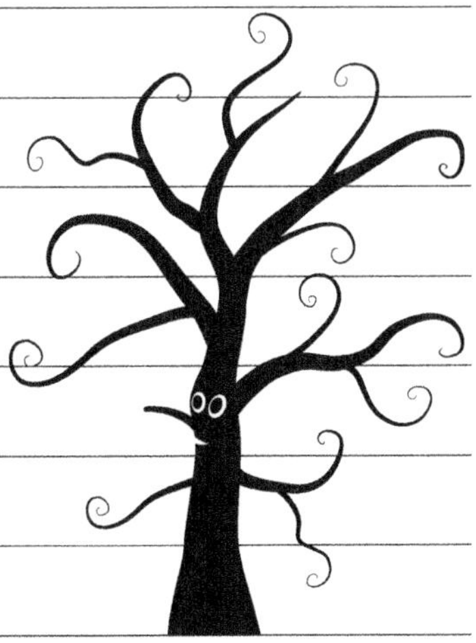

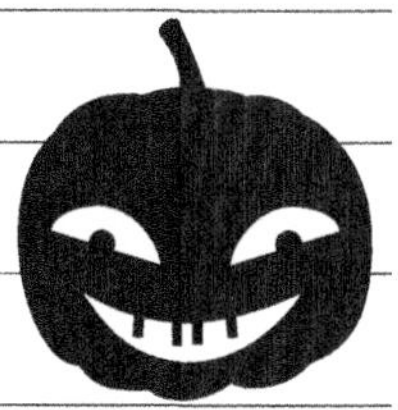

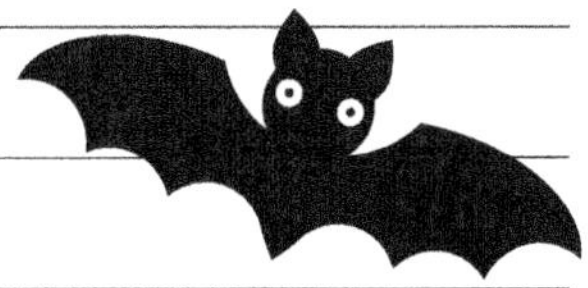

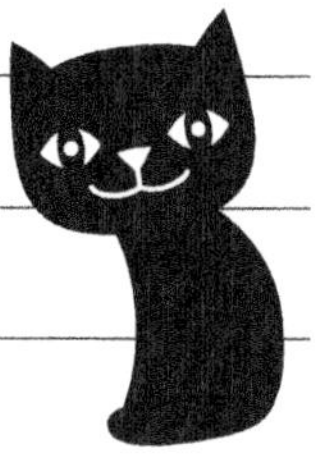

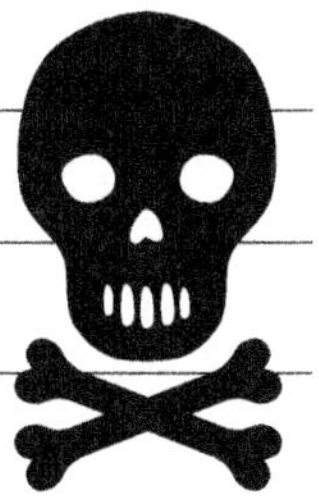

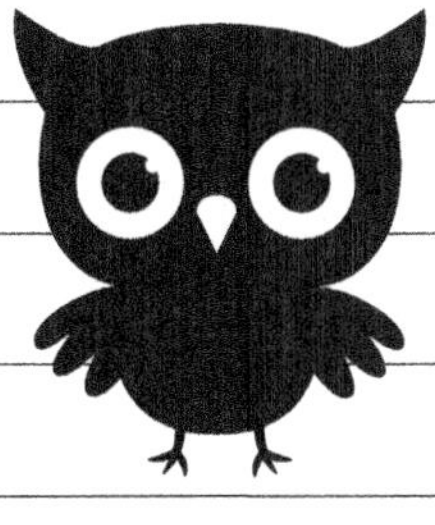

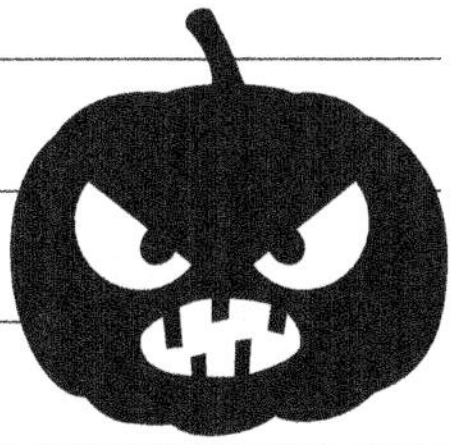

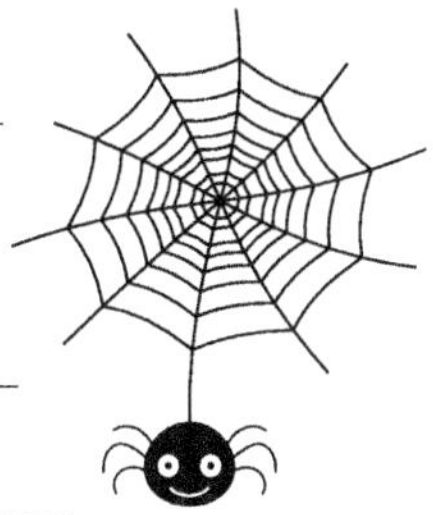

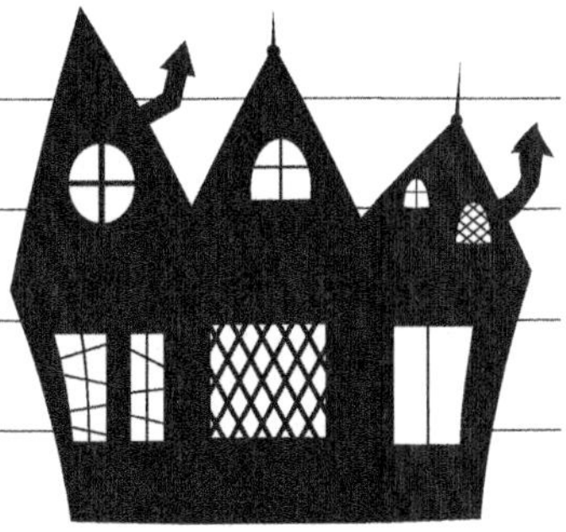

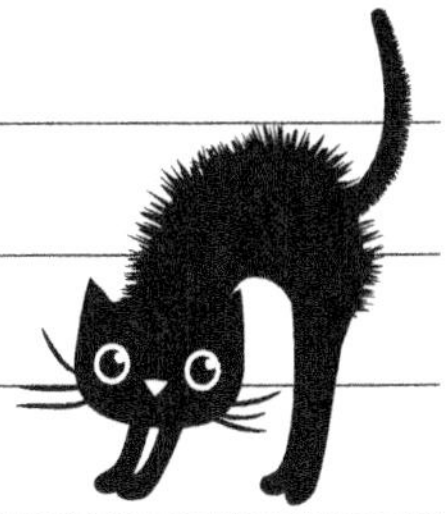

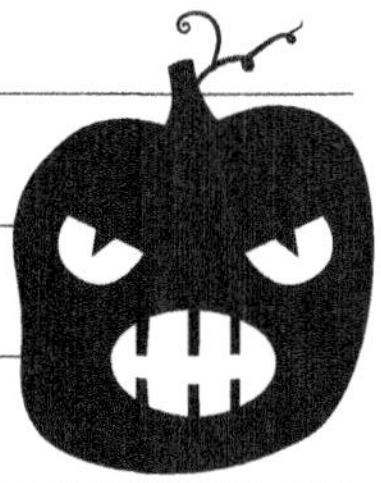

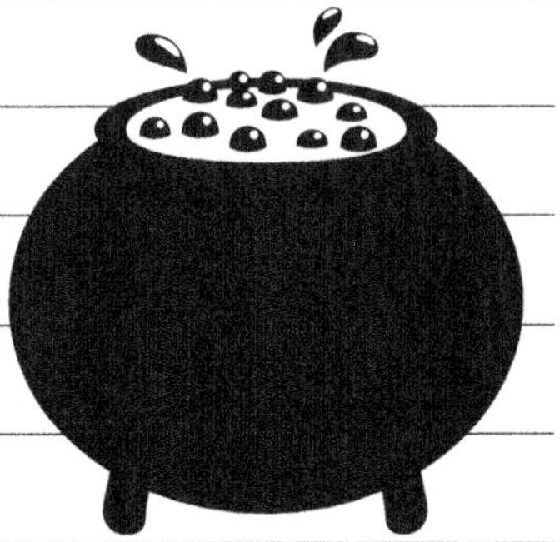

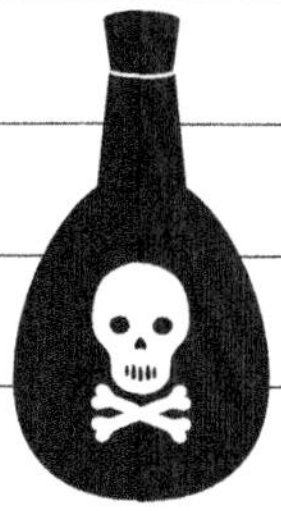

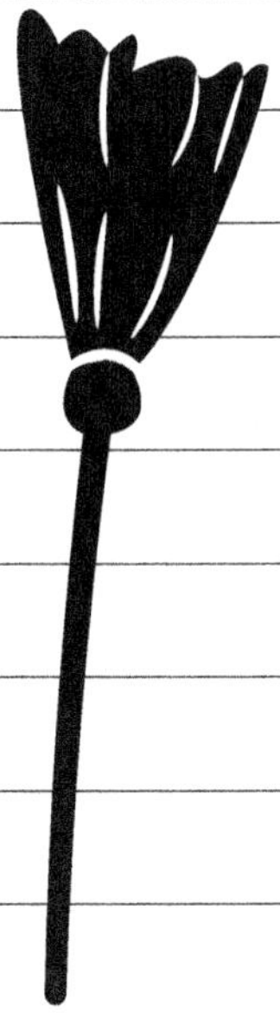

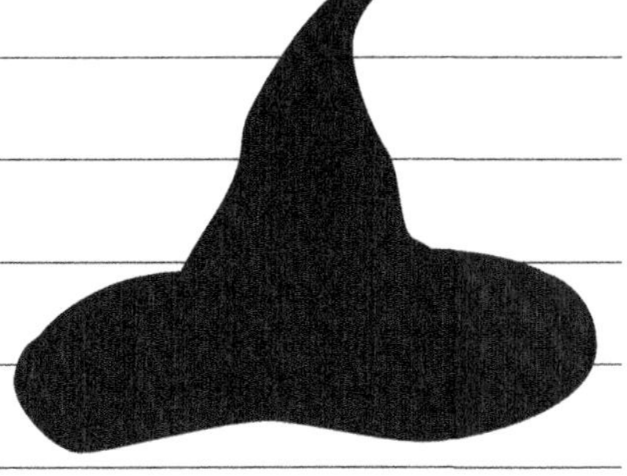

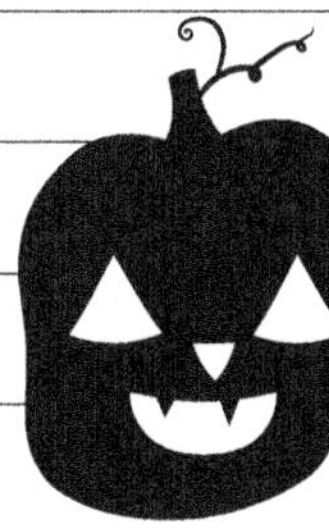

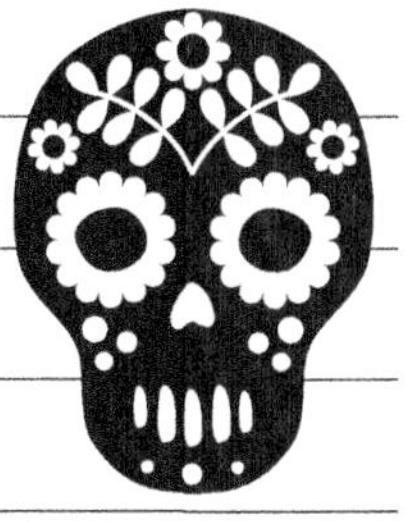

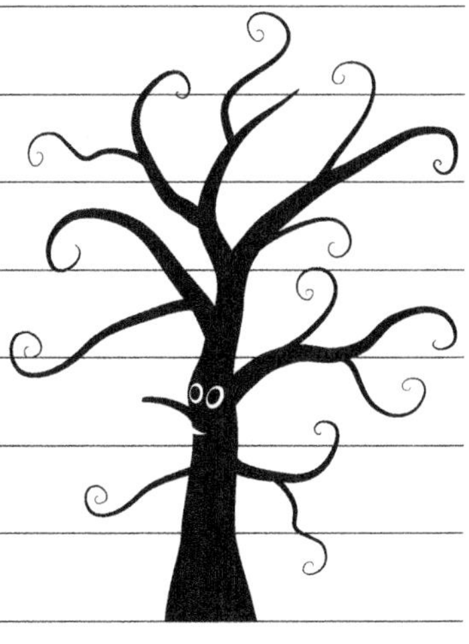

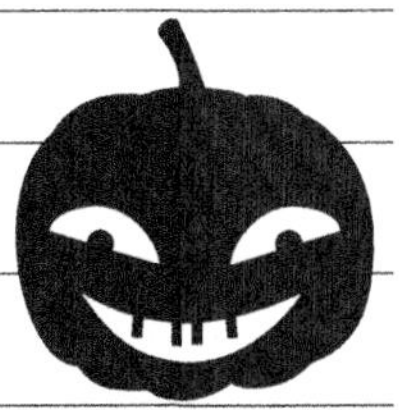

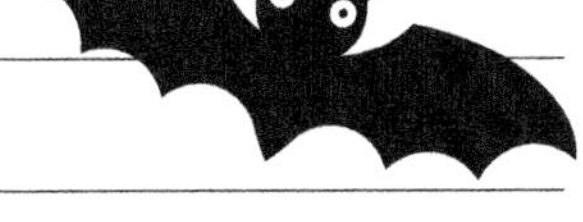

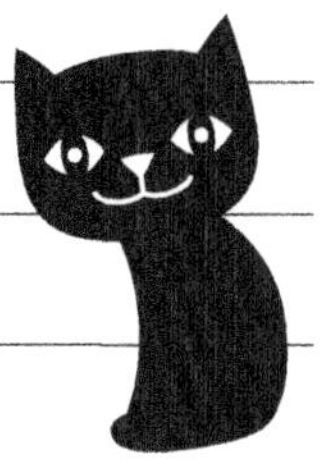

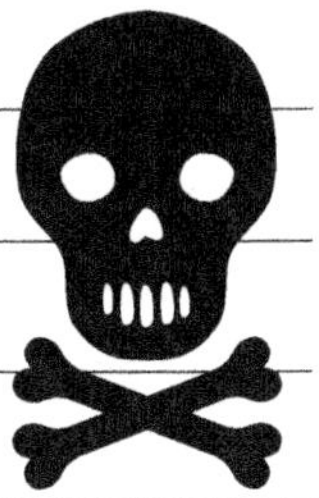

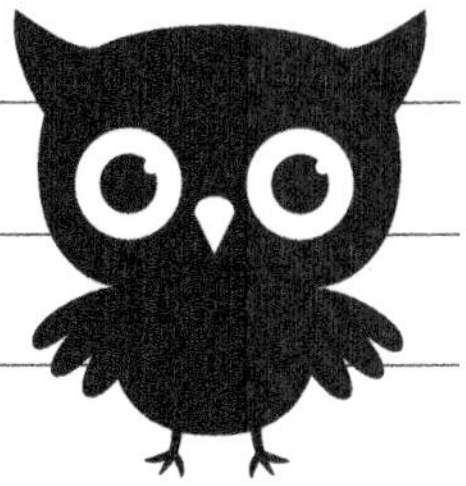

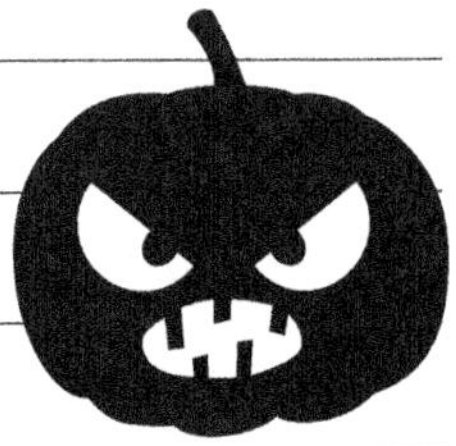

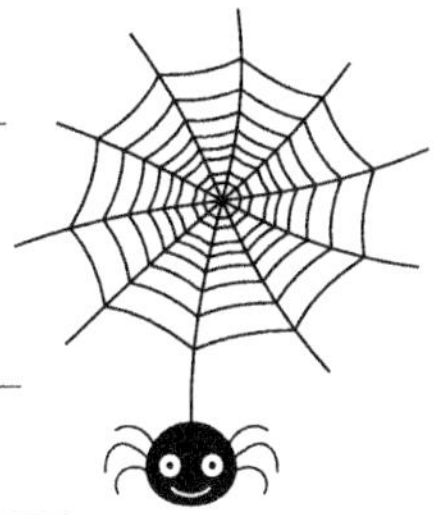

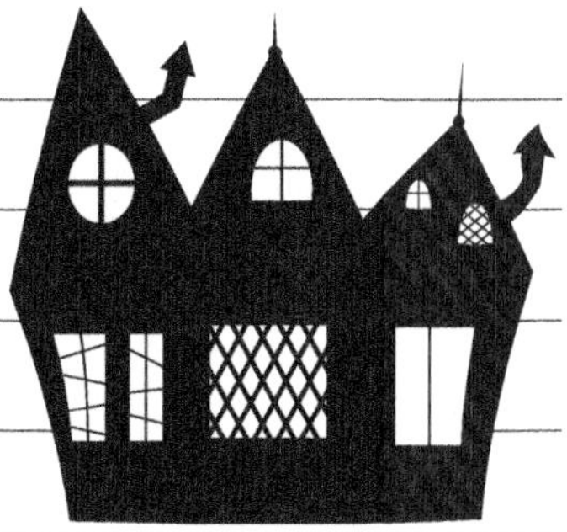

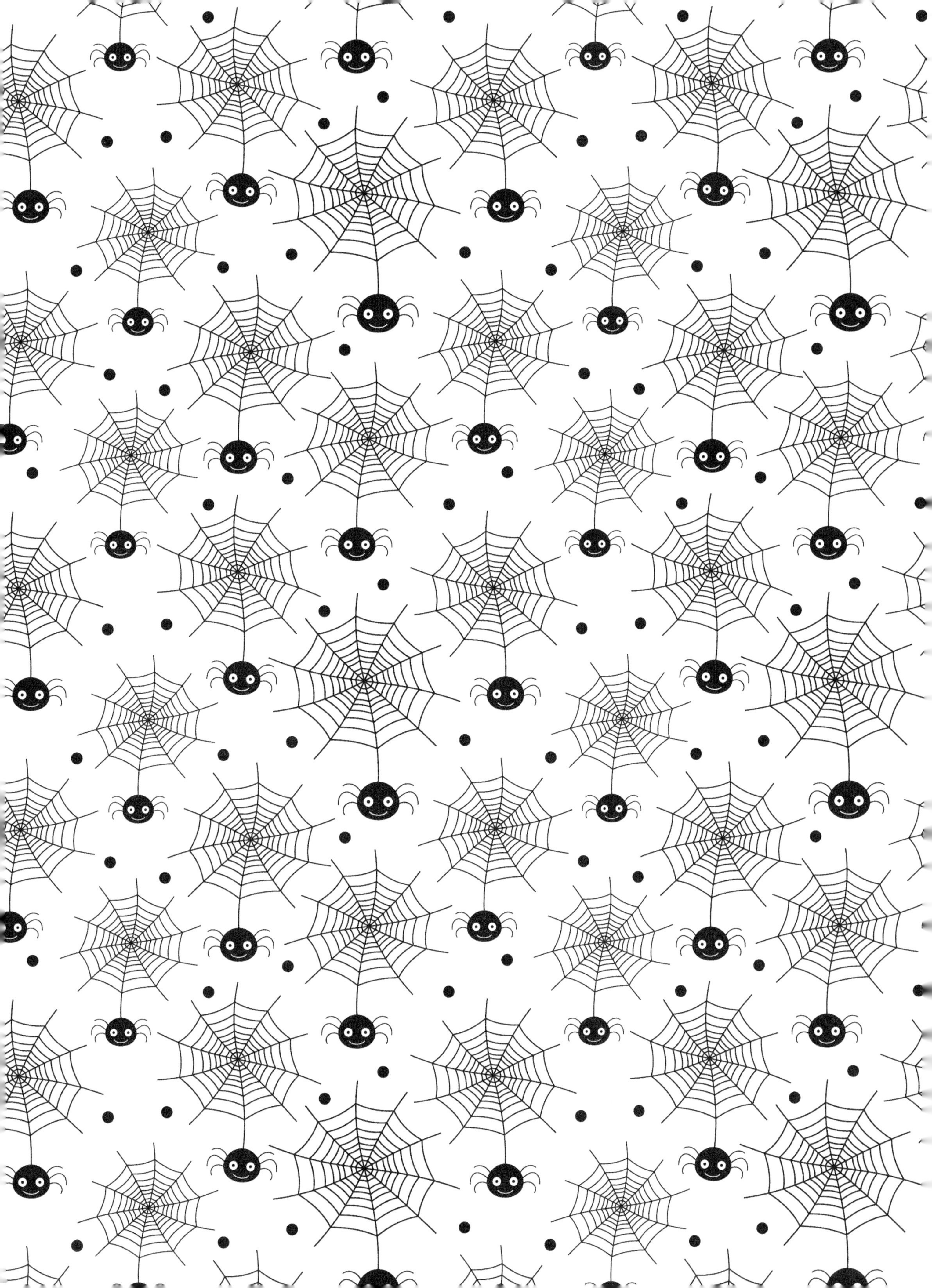

Printed in Great Britain
by Amazon

32227048R00057